The Explorer's Path:
A Map for Practical Anti-Nihilism

by
Sulien Valentino Solovyov

The Explorer's Path: A Map for Practical Anti-Nihilism
by Sulien Valentino Solovyov
ISBN: 978-1-989647-89-9
First published November 1, 2025
Toronto, Ontario

Publisher: The Evergreen Centre

Publisher's Cataloging-in-Publication Data
Sulien Valentino Solovyov

The Explorer's Path: A Map for Practical Anti-Nihilism / First edition.

Summary: A philosophical and practical guide that challenges the pervasive modern culture of distraction and meaninglessness by providing a structured path for rediscovering purpose. It introduces the use of focused, sensory acts—such as cooking elemental foods and listening to intentional music—as a daily liturgy to rebuild the soul's interior architecture and ground abstract truths in physical reality.

Identifiers: ISBN 978-1-989647-89-9

Subjects: Philosophy, Practical. | Spiritual life. | Ethics. | Self-Help—Intentionality. | Contemplative practice.

Classification: 170—dc23

The Explorer's Path:
A Map for Practical Anti-Nihilism

by
Sulien Valentino Solovyov

Letter to the Reader

There are moments when life feels flattened—when the world hums with noise but not with meaning. Screens glow, headlines spin, and somewhere between our morning routines and late-night scrolling, the question returns: what for?

If you are holding this little book, you have likely asked it too. Perhaps not aloud, but inwardly—at the sight of cruelty that passes for cleverness, or in the dull ache that follows achievement. We live in an age of acceleration, yet our hearts lag behind. The result is not enlightenment, but exhaustion.

This book is a small map drawn from larger roads. It is not an argument so much as a series of waystations—texts and lives that mark the passage from disorientation toward order, from cynicism toward care. You will meet philosophers and poets, saints and skeptics, detectives and bakers. Each has glimpsed some fragment of the True, the Good, or the Beautiful, and each offers a lamp for the traveler who refuses despair.

I write not as a scholar but as a fellow pilgrim, one who has also wrestled with silence and distraction. What follows is a path traced through those wrestlings—a way of rebuilding the soul's interior architecture, stone by stone, grace by grace.

You need not believe everything here. You need only walk a little way. The map will clarify as you move, and if you keep your eyes lifted, you may find that even the smallest acts—the prayer, the gesture, the loaf of bread—begin to glow with significance again. That is the promise of this path: that meaning, once lost, can be made visible by love.

—The Author

To Reclaim Ground: A Rooted Guide for the Introduction

The Hearth (Cooking/Baking)	The Soundtrack (Instrumental)
Make:	Listen:
Irish Soda Bread: Simple and immediate, reflecting an unadorned, foundational attempt at structure and comfort when the soul feels "unmoored."	**John Cage, 4'33":** Forces confrontation with ambient sound and silence—the ultimate elemental act of beginning.
White Bean Dip: Elemental and adaptable, embodying sustenance and humility; a clear, accessible first step.	**J.S. Bach, Cello Suite No. 1 in G Major, Prelude:** Stable, rational order.
Cream of Mushroom Soup with Endive: The earthy "ground" of the soup meets the sharp, bitter "counterpoint" of the endive, gently hinting at the complexity of the problem.	**Bill Evans, Peace Piece / Thelonious Monk, Reflections:** Quiet, reflective jazz for contemplation.

Introduction:
The Problem of the Unmoored Soul

This is not a book about politics, history, or the latest cultural war. This is a book about gravity.

For too many of us, the twenty-first century feels like a condition of weightlessness.

Our lives are faster, richer, and technically more connected than any civilization before, yet we feel profoundly unmoored. We wake up in houses filled with technology, surrounded by people, and equipped with limitless access to information, only to find our inner lives characterized by a low-grade, persistent feeling of drift.

The modern malaise is not hunger; it is thirst. We are not suffering from a lack of stimuli; we are drowning in it.

The primary human crisis is no longer external survival, but internal orientation.

We have forgotten
where we are,
who we are,
and

what
we are
for.

This loss of moral and spiritual gravity leaves the soul fragmented, anxious, and perpetually waiting for an external event to provide the meaning only an internal anchor can supply.

This journey is an effort to find that anchor. It is a pilgrimage back to first principles, designed to restore the essential coordinates that define a whole, purposeful, and rightly ordered life.

The Digital Ditch: Drowning and Thirsting

Look around you. We live in an age of distraction, where constant, trivial stimuli are mistaken for genuine experience. Our attention is the last, great frontier of human freedom, and it is being colonized minute by minute. We carry devices that connect us to everyone else, but often disconnect us entirely from our own immediate reality—from the feel of the sunlight, the conversation across the table, or the quiet pulse of our own thoughts.

This environment creates a stark paradox: We drown in stimuli but thirst for meaning.

We have fallen into the **Digital Ditch**—a self-dug hole lined with infinite content. We believe that if we just consume one more article, watch one more video, or answer one more notification, we will finally catch up to the truth, or achieve a sense of completeness. But this consumption is corrosive. It hollows out the attention, leaving us perpetually exhausted and fundamentally dissatisfied.

The world provides so many maps, charts, and data points that we forget to look up at the actual stars. We are addicted to the noise of the world because the noise is often easier to bear than the terrifying silence of our own unaddressed interior life.

This is the central problem of the **unmoored soul**: The refusal to be still, because stillness reveals the lack of internal structure.

The Pilgrim's Map: A School for Sanity
This book is an invitation to leave the ditch and begin a **pilgrimage**.

A pilgrimage is not a vacation; it is a journey of intentional transformation. It is a temporary commitment to hardship and focus designed to recalibrate your relationship with yourself and the world.

The pages ahead serve as your **Pilgrim's Map.** It is not a prescription for absolute perfection, but a guide designed to bring you into contact with the foundational ideas that sustain sanity:

Chapter 1 (The Foundational Ascent): We begin by restoring wonder, humility, and the rational order of self-mastery. We learn to breathe clean air again.

Chapter 2 (Navigating the Abyss): We then confront the deepest errors—pride, fragmentation, and the nihilistic temptation—to understand why our souls feel hollowed out.

Chapter 3 (Knights Errant): We seek out models of embodied courage, learning how justice and fidelity are practiced in a cynical, lawless world.

Chapter 4 (Reclaiming Ground): We move from theory to action, discovering how purpose is built, not found, in the daily, incarnational acts of home, work, and redemptive suffering.

The entire journey becomes a school for sanity—a sustained exercise in returning the fractured modern consciousness to its natural, steady state.

A Word on the Compass: Coordinates of Truth

To begin walking, we must first set our **Compass**. The great error of the unmoored soul is the belief that meaning is something to be invented or purchased. True meaning is found by aligning oneself with enduring, external coordinates of truth.

The journey ahead will guide us back to three simple, essential coordinates:

Grace (The Unearned Gift): This is the Chestertonian concept that existence itself is an unearned miracle. It is the necessary humility that breaks the cycle of boredom and entitlement. Without acknowledging the unearned gift, we can only be critics, never creators.

Conscience (The Internal Law): This is the rational conscience that C.S. Lewis and Dostoevsky force us to confront. It is the recognition that the moral law is not a social contract, but the operational manual for the human heart. To violate it is to violate your own integrity.

The Dignity of Labor (Vocation): This is the Frankl-inspired, Beard-embodied truth that we find purpose by actively giving of ourselves through creation and service. The integrity of a life is measured not by its consumption, but by the tangible gifts it produces.

We are not setting off to discover new continents. We are undertaking the far harder journey: **to find our way back home, back to the simple, enduring truths that have held humanity in place for millennia.**

A Note on Intentionality: How to Use This Book

This is not a book to be rushed. It is a series of waystations on a pilgrimage, and the map will only clarify if you walk slowly. Please approach the content one chapter at a time, treating the ideas not as arguments, but as prompts for practice.

The first section of every chapter, "To Reclaim Ground," is your practical guide. The Hearth (Food) and the Soundtrack (Music) are not mere suggestions for ambiance. They are tools for presence–a deliberate, small liturgy designed to fight the age of distraction. By engaging your hands in the preparation of an elemental food, or by anchoring your mind to the intentional rhythm of the music, you create an interior order before reading.

This is the central task: to transition the act of reading from an abstract mental task into a grounded, incarnational act of the soul. Put on the music, prepare the bite, and only then, begin to read.

To Reclaim Ground: A Rooted Guide for Chapter 1

The Hearth (Cooking/Baking)	The Soundtrack (Instrumental)
Make:	Listen:
Black Cowboy Coffee: Stark, black, and potent, symbolizing unwavering focus and pure energy for the journey.	**Classical: J.S. Bach - Goldberg Variations, Aria:** The ultimate Baroque foundation. Pure, elegant, and perfectly balanced, representing the structure upon which the Heart and Compass are set.
Texas Breakfast Hash Chili with Hatch Chiles: A rugged, intensely flavored, and satisfying dish that offers both fortitude and heat (drive/willpower).	**Classical: Joaquín Rodrigo - Concierto de Aranjuez, Adagio:** The haunting, deep, and emotional melody provides the "Heart" needed for the Ascent—a passionate yet controlled spiritual searching.
Ashcakes with Honey and Cayenne: The ultimate elemental food, representing the most basic, humble foundation. Honey provides pure energy, and Cayenne symbolizes the necessary fire or intensity of the "Ascent."	**Jazz / Instrumental: Paul Winter Consort - "Icarus":** An expansive piece of spiritual-modal jazz representing the stretching toward a goal and setting the compass toward something higher and aspirational.

To Reclaim Ground: A Rooted Guide for Chapter 1 (cont.)

The Hearth (Cooking/Baking)

The Soundtrack (Instrumental)

Make:

Listen:

Aged Asiago Wedge and Toasted Walnuts: Structured, pure, and high-quality; the intense, crystalline flavor reflects the precision and clarity of the Towner piece and the Stoic mindset.	**Jazz / Instrumental: Ralph Towner - "Solstice"** (from the album *Solstice*): An introspective, acoustic piece defined by lyrical clarity and compositional precision, reflecting the intelligent structure of the Stoic ascent.
Square of Olive Oil Cake: Moist, aromatic, and deeply satisfying; its ancient, humble Mediterranean nature reflects the deep roots of wisdom and provides gentle, sustained energy and hope.	**Jazz / Instrumental: Vince Guaraldi - "Cast Your Fate to the Wind":** A lyrical, hopeful melody suggesting trust and forward momentum.

Chapter 1 – The Foundational Ascent
Setting the Heart and Compass

The feeling is unmistakable. It is the deep, steadying breath taken on a mountain peak after a long, choked climb out of a valley. It is the sudden, complete return of gravity—not as a burden, but as the great, reliable law that holds the cosmos together. For too long, we have lived as astronauts cut from their tether, drifting in a silent, overwhelming blackness. We have mistaken that vertigo for freedom.

We are here to recover the anchor. We are here to rebuild the interior order, stone by stone, until the world outside becomes intelligible again.

The work of a lifetime is not to rearrange the world to suit your whims, but to arrange yourself so that you can see the world as it truly is.

Wonder as Sanity
(Chesterton, Orthodoxy)

The descent into meaninglessness is rarely a sudden plunge;
it is a slow, quiet freezing of the senses.

It begins when we confuse familiarity with necessity.

We look out at the world—at the regular swing of the seasons,
the unvarying beat of our own heart, the daily unrelenting return
of the sunrise—and we conclude that these are not miracles, but
mere mechanisms.

This is the precise moment when the fever of distraction spikes,
and the long, low illness of the modern soul takes hold.

We are here to administer the cure, and that cure is found in the simple, towering sanity of G.K. Chesterton. He saw existence not as a dull furniture-set but as a gift perpetually renewed.

The philosophical disease of the age is not doubt; it is boredom. It is the breathtaking arrogance of surveying the cosmos and saying, "I've seen it all before."

To be sane is to treat existence not as a debt that is owed, but as an endlessly surprising party you were somehow invited to.

This sense of exhaustion, of finding everything uninteresting, is profoundly irrational. It requires a complex, elaborate, and ultimately exhausting network of assumptions to dismiss the sky as merely blue, or the human mind as merely complex chemistry.

The child, the true philosopher, looks at the green grass and is astonished that it is green, not purple. The modern adult looks at it and is annoyed that it is not green enough. The poet sees a law; the cynic sees a chain.

Our task is to cultivate gratitude to the point of intellectual rigor.

Every breath taken, every functioning neuron, every law of gravity that holds your cup to the table is an unearned reprieve.

We must not mistake the reliability of the universe for its banality. The sun rises again not because it must, but because it is given permission, an encore performance of staggering scale. This is not sentimentality; it is the truest, clearest sight.

The first, fundamental law of recovering meaning is therefore an act of humility.

We must bow to the reality that we are not the authors of this play, but the highly privileged audience members. When the Heart resets, it doesn't beat faster; it beats with a sudden, powerful stillness. We regain the confidence mixed with wonder that proclaims: The world is intelligible again.

The Discipline of Fortitude
(Epictetus, Discourses)

Joy requires a foundation of granite. The sheer delight of Chestertonian wonder can quickly dissolve into chaos if it is not supported by the hard, clear-eyed philosophy of Epictetus. He stands as our companion in sanity, the philosopher-teacher whose wisdom was forged in the chains of slavery and thus speaks with unassailable authority on true freedom.

The essence of the discipline is a ruthless, daily triage of attention. We must learn to cleave reality in two with a single, sharp inquiry:

What is within my power, and what is not?

We spend a ruinous amount of emotional capital wrestling with ghosts: the future we cannot predict, the past we cannot undo, the opinions we cannot control, and the choices of others that we cannot dictate. Every attempt to force these externals to conform to our desires is a willful surrender of our interior order. We volunteer for slavery the moment we tie our peace of mind to an event outside the walls of our own consciousness.

First say to yourself what you would be; and then do what you have to do. The mastery of self precedes the mastery of the world. **The Discipline of Fortitude** is the daily, grinding effort to make the single territory you own—your judgment, your will, and your reaction—**an unbreachable fortress**. This is not about being cold or uncaring; it is about being strategically stable. When a slight is offered, your response is not a reflex but a deliberate choice. When an inconvenience strikes, your internal state does not wobble; it maintains its center of balance. This intentionality, this cultivation of the inner assent, is where all genuine power resides. We are seeking physical stability as a metaphor for moral order.

Think of a sailor on a pitching deck. The waves are chaos. The wind is unpredictable. His job is not to stop the storm, but to root his own body so deeply—to brace his stance, to keep his center of gravity low—that he can act with precision amidst the madness. This rooting is Fortitude. It is the unyielding resolve to maintain equilibrium under duress.

When you master your attention, you gain more time, more energy, and more clarity than any external achievement could ever grant. The compass needle, once spun wildly by every passing opinion, now settles, points true, and holds fast. This disciplined humility—the clear-eyed acknowledgement of our true sphere of influence—is the very basis for any meaningful recovery.

Harmony Before Control
(Lao Tzu, Tao Te Ching)

The Stoic discipline gave us an unshakable core. But a well-ordered interior is not the end of the journey; it is merely the ship's hull, ready for the water. The next crucial step in our foundational ascent is to learn how to sail. This requires shedding the exhausting Western impulse to force the world into submission and embracing the effortless power of Harmony.

We turn now to the quiet wisdom of Lao Tzu, the philosopher who saw the great cosmic intelligence not as a demanding monarch, but as a flowing river—the Tao.

The modern disease is the worship of Control. We believe meaning is found in imposing our will upon reality. We see the world as clay to be molded, an adversary to be conquered. This relentless, aggressive posture is what leaves us perpetually exhausted and brittle. When you push against the current, you are guaranteed resistance. When you try to hold water in a clenched fist, you lose it entirely.

The greatest power is to become ungraspable, yielding, and essential.

This is the principle of Wu Wei, often translated as "non-action" or "effortless action." It is not laziness; it is an intelligent humility. It means acting in alignment with the nature of things, rather than fighting against them. Think of the expert fisherman who doesn't wrestle the river, but simply knows where to cast his line. He doesn't exert more force; he applies the correct force at the correct time, allowing the inherent logic of the system to do the heavy lifting.

This wisdom is profoundly rational. When we cease trying to micromanage every outcome, we free up vast stores of mental energy. We learn to observe the natural patterns of our work, our relationships, and our own inner life, then step into the current at the moment of least resistance. The pivotal insight here is that we retain absolute agency in choosing the current—discerning which streams are healthy and productive, and precisely why we wish to join them. With this disciplined core, we then release, observe, and react with intention.

The world, when you cease trying to control it, begins to feel less like a battlefield and more like a great, ongoing conversation.

The way to master the world is not to grasp, but to release.

To find our moral ease, we must learn to release the need for constant control, trusting the chosen current to carry us. Our efforts then become quieter, deeper, and infinitely more effective, as we align with the natural patterns of the world. This profound balance—this effortless resting in the system of the Tao—is what we must cultivate in our souls.

This doesn't mean passively drifting. Rather, through careful observation within the current, we gain the wisdom to discern new paths and, at any point, make the conscious choice to step out and embark on a different journey. Even the stream need not be our final destination or defining companion. Unless it is.

When we move with the Tao, we begin to hear the sound of the world working for us, rather than against us. Our Compass is now set not by the frantic pull of ego, but by the quiet magnetism of the whole.

The Virtue of Routine
(Benjamin Franklin, Autobiography)

We have established the Heart in wonder (Chesterton) and anchored the Compass in self-mastery (Epictetus) and flow (Lao Tzu). But these are high-altitude concepts. They need a landing strip. They must be woven into the fabric of daily life, or they will remain beautiful, useless abstractions.

Our final guide on this foundational ascent is the most earthbound and pragmatic of all: Benjamin Franklin. His great philosophical contribution wasn't in grand treatises, but in his meticulous, almost obsessive commitment to order and routine, as detailed in his Autobiography.

Franklin understood a profound, liberating paradox: Order is freedom.

We often view routine as a form of intellectual imprisonment—a dull repetition that stifles spontaneity. We believe freedom lies in absolute, unstructured choice. This is a mirage. Unstructured choice leads not to liberation, but to decision fatigue, anxiety, and the steady erosion of valuable time. The person who has to decide what to eat, what to wear, and when to work every single day is the one who is truly enslaved by the trivial.

Build the stable scaffolding of your life first, so that your mind can be free to scale the heights.

Franklin's famous attempt to cultivate Thirteen Virtues—temperance, silence, order, resolution, among others—was not about achieving puritanical perfection.

It was a rational strategy for cognitive load management. By systematizing the ordinary, he created mental space for the extraordinary. His daily schedule, his methodical approach to self-improvement, was simply the construction of a highly efficient internal machine designed to produce great works.
Think of an athlete. Their freedom to perform a spontaneous, elegant move on the field is not a result of ignoring discipline; it is the direct result of years of rutted routine. The fundamentals are so deeply ingrained in muscle memory that the conscious mind is liberated to improvise. Routine is the path to mastery without thought.

This is our sensory grounding made practical. We are seeking moral and intellectual stability. Just as a sturdy house requires a foundation poured level and square, so too does a life of meaning require a schedule that is dependable and intentional.
Start small. Establish a deliberate routine for the first two hours of your day. Protect your mornings. Begin with a single act of disciplined silence, followed by a focused task. This is the physical ritual that reminds your mind and body that you are in charge of the day's direction, not its passing whims.

This daily construction of order is the final, essential act of humility and fortitude, demonstrating that you are ready not just to think great thoughts, but to live a great life.

To Reclaim Ground: A Rooted Guide for Chapter 2

The Hearth (Cooking/Baking)	The Soundtrack (Instrumental)
Make:	Listen:
"Burnt Ends" (Intensely Charred Brisket/Pork Belly): Intensely smoky and caramelized, a culinary metaphor for darkness, complexity, and a brutal, compelling flavor profile	**Bartók, Music for Strings, Percussion and Celesta, Movement II (Allegro):** A dissonant, driving fugue that symbolizes existential anxiety and chaotic internal psychological struggle.
Charred Roasted Beet: Maintains a dark, earthy color and flavor profile, providing a deeply grounded base flavor that aligns with confronting fundamental existence.	**Shostakovich, String Quartet No. 8, Movement I (Largo):** Deeply personal, mournful, and dominated by the D-S-C-H motif, capturing profound, crushing despair (fitting for Raskolnikov).
Dark Rye Bread with Molasses and Black Currants: The molasses adds a tar-like color and deep sweetness, reflecting the 'shadows,' with currants symbolizing small, challenging glimmers of complexity.	**Pat Metheny and Ornette Coleman, "Song X":** Angular, dense avant-garde jazz embodying the clash of order and chaos (Nietzsche's theme).

Chapter 2 – Navigating the Abyss
Shadows of Meaninglessness

If the first chapter was the clearing of the air, this one is the descent into the chamber where the air first grew stale. To rebuild the house, we must understand the forces that caused the collapse. We must confront the anatomy of our despair, the structures of our self-deception, and the deep, fracturing errors that lead the soul into its own private shadowlands.

The great temptation of the modern age is not simple wickedness; it is fragmentation. We have detached the intellect from the heart, the will from the compass, and the self from the sustaining fabric of transcendent law. We must now diagnose the specific pathologies born of this separation.

The descent is necessary. You cannot recover what you refuse to name.

Reason Without Conscience
(Fyodor Dostoevsky, Crime and Punishment)

The first shadow we must confront is the most chilling because it is cast by our own intellectual light. It is the seductive error of hyper-rationalism—the belief that the mind, severed from any external moral constraint, is competent to define its own laws. We find the perfect, terrifying laboratory for this idea in the protagonist of Fyodor Dostoevsky's masterpiece, **Crime and Punishment: Raskolnikov**. He is the ultimate intellectual criminal, not motivated by need or passion, but by a meticulously constructed theory. He argues that certain 'extraordinary men' have the right—even the duty—to step over conventional morality, to commit a small sin for a great purpose. He uses Reason as a scalpel to excise Conscience.

The horror of the story is not the act itself, but its psychological aftermath. The great, cold, rational experiment immediately fails. Raskolnikov is not liberated; he is alienated. The moment he elevates his own intellect as the sole measure of good and bad, he cuts himself off from the very humanity he was supposedly trying to save. His guilt becomes not a product of societal condemnation, but a terrifying, self-generated psychic torture.

Intellect, when it defines its own law, builds a palace of isolation. The walls are constructed not of brick, but of relentless, justifying logic, and the only occupant is the architect himself, condemned to endless self-assessment. He finds that this self-made solitude is not the throne of the Superman he sought to occupy, but a barren, airtight cell. The world outside the mind—the world of simple, shared suffering and common grace—becomes opaque, muffled, and irrelevant. The theory was meant to ascend above the herd; the reality is an abyss that separates him from the simplest act of connection.

This is the great, undeniable diagnosis: Reason without grace is a tool of magnificent, self-destructive precision. It can justify anything, but it can redeem nothing. *When the intellect refuses to acknowledge any wisdom higher than its own calculations, it inevitably concludes that it is God.*

The consequence is not empowerment, but a desolate and absolute guilt. The air grows thick, and the light of truth cannot penetrate the meticulously reasoned walls of the self.

The moment he tries to calculate a life—to balance the ledger of one small crime against a thousand calculated good deeds—he finds that the ledger refuses to close. The human heart, stubbornly illogical, will not accept the tyranny of the brain's arithmetic. Logic is revealed as a desert, capable of sustaining neither morality nor meaning. The true sin of Raskolnikov is not murder; it is the reduction of existence to a problem that can be solved by a single, brilliant mind.

And the final, terrifying realization is that the problem, once solved, yields no happiness, only the hollow echo of a system that has devoured its own foundations.

The consequence of his theoretical freedom is the absolute collapse of his soul's infrastructure.

Against Raskolnikov's towering, self-inflicted isolation stands Sonia. Her wisdom is not reasoned; it is received. Where he sought liberation through logical transgression, she lives by constant, quiet self-sacrifice, a profound wellspring of unconditional self-giving.

Her truth resides not in individual will, but in the simple, profound act of bearing witness and sharing the burden. She offers the only antidote to his fractured intellect: love without condition or expectation.

It is this uncalculating love that cracks the walls of his reasoned prison. Sonia offers no new philosophy, but a living example of radical humility and compassion. She reveals the fatal flaw in Raskolnikov's edifice of logic: it has no language for the broken heart, no calculus for shared redemption.

Through her, a different path emerges: not individual genius, but the reunion with **a sacred, universal order.** The way out of isolation is found not through another brilliant thought, but through the terrifying, liberating act of bowing down. Her suffering, embraced and offered, becomes the bridge back into the stream of humanity he abandoned.

The Haunting Mind
(Edgar Allan Poe, The Tell-Tale Heart)

The consequence of Raskolnikov's intellectual crime—the chilling experiment of reason divorced from grace, where the individual intellect assumes sole divine authority—is not merely societal; it is internal and terrifyingly intimate. Having dismissed external law, we find that the judge, the jury, and the executioner all remain—and they reside within. The self becomes its own tormentor, trapped in an inescapable courtroom of its own making.

Edgar Allan Poe understood the limits of a purely internal moral judge with chilling clarity. In The Tell-Tale Heart, the narrator meticulously plans and executes a perfect murder, believing his superior intellect has accounted for every possibility. Yet, in the aftermath, the haunting begins. He hears the rhythmic, unbearable pounding of the murdered man's heart.

This isn't a supernatural phenomenon. It is a profound psychological truth: the moral self is indelible. When we try to bury the law, the law does not vanish; it simply becomes a part of our own fractured psyche, a relentless, deafening rhythm demanding recognition. The sound the narrator hears is not the old man's heart; it is the pounding of his own severed conscience, screaming from the depths of its forced interment.

There is no exit from the self if the self is the source of its own law. Poe strips away all societal consequence to reveal the raw, terrifying limit of the purely internal judge. Guilt, when denied, does not dissipate; it becomes a haunting, fixed, and paranoid obsession. The light of clarity is replaced by a nervous, flickering torchlight that illuminates only the dark corners of one's own paranoia, never revealing the way out.

This is the truth of moral fragmentation: the mind that rejects external order, that insists on its own solitary legislation, ultimately becomes a self-contained, self-cannibalizing abyss. It is the ultimate irony: the pursuit of absolute freedom through intellectual autonomy leads directly to the most absolute and inescapable form of spiritual bondage. The grand, logical design collapses inward, leaving only the echo of a heart that refuses to be silenced, and a mind eternally condemned by its own, solitary decree.

The Idol of the Will
(Friedrich Nietzsche, Beyond Good and Evil)

The apex of this fragmentation—the full-throated rejection of external constraint—is articulated by Friedrich Nietzsche. His philosophy confronts us with a magnificent, terrifying temptation: the **Idol of the Will**.

Nietzsche's great diagnosis was the death of God, which he understood would inevitably lead to nihilism. His solution was the creation of the **Übermensch**—the individual who, recognizing the abyss, chooses to become the measure of all things. This is the **Will to Power**: the impulse to seize control, to deify self-created strength, and to legislate morality from the seat of one's own autonomy.

This philosophy is brutally honest and powerfully seductive. It tells us that our strength lies in our refusal to be bound by anything inherited or external. But this absolute autonomy is a trap. For at the heart of humanity lies the '**Will to Theosis**'—the inherent drive towards ultimate union, towards participating in something greater than the isolated self. When the Will to Power, in its radical self-assertion, refuses to acknowledge even this deepest origin— its language, its history, its very existence as a cultural artifact—it inevitably collapses into the solipsistic despair of the ego.

When the individual Will becomes the highest good, it is left without an anchor, constantly driven to re-create itself in a vacuum. It offers a glorious moment of intellectual pride, but this quickly yields to the deep terror of knowing that the meaning you created today can be uncreated tomorrow. This self-made meaning, untethered from any shared or transcendent source, is ultimately fragile, prone to dissolving with the shifting sands of individual caprice. The very act of asserting absolute autonomy paradoxically creates an existential treadmill, a perpetual, exhausting striving to fill a void that only grows larger with each attempted self-definition.

Nietzsche's abyss is the space where the Will to Power, having killed God, finds itself unable to sustain its own divinity. It discovers, in that terrifying freedom, not liberation, but an unending burden. The void left by the absence of a higher truth is not filled by self-generated values; it merely echoes with the clamor of a solitary will desperate to convince itself of its own ultimate significance.

This is the profound, tragic irony: the heroic effort to transcend all external authority ultimately leads to a prison of the self, where meaning must be ceaselessly manufactured and defended against its own inherent instability. The yearning for Theosis—for union and ultimate belonging—is brutally suppressed, only to manifest as a relentless, unquenchable thirst for power that can never truly satisfy, for it seeks to become that which it simultaneously denies. The self, attempting to become God, succeeds only in becoming a god of its own desolate, self-consuming universe.

The Will to Fidelity
(Thomas à Kempis, The Imitation of Christ)

To confront this ultimate nihilistic temptation, we must immediately pivot to the antidote—a quiet, enduring wisdom that offers the true path of transcendence. We place the aggressive, self-deifying Will to Power directly against the humble, stabilizing **Will to Fidelity** as illuminated by Thomas à Kempis in The Imitation of Christ. This is the active, conscious embrace of our deepest longing for Theosis—for union and participation in a reality far greater than our isolated ego.

Where Nietzsche demands that we create our own law, à Kempis demonstrates the courageous freedom found in choosing alignment with an enduring, external truth. This is not a philosophy of weakness, but of profound, stabilizing strength.

It begins with a radical shift in perspective: from viewing external order as a constraint to recognizing it as **the very architecture of true liberty**. The ego, accustomed to its throne, recoils from this initial surrender, mistaking humility for diminishment. Yet, it is precisely in this voluntary offering of self-will that the boundless expanse of genuine freedom is discovered.

The true **Will to Transcendence** is not self-creation; it is the courageous choice of submission—a complete surrender of the ego's demands to a higher, more complete design (the Word of God). This isn't a coerced subjugation, but an intelligent, deliberate act of alignment, a recognition that the universe functions by principles greater than our fleeting desires. It is a profound, practical discipline:

1. Practically, it means **cultivating an ear for wisdom beyond our own thoughts**. It means actively seeking the deep currents of perennial truths that echo through time, rather than only listening to the clamor of our immediate desires or the latest intellectual fashions.

2. It requires **a daily, conscious redirection of the will**. When the ego insists on its own logic, we gently, but firmly, reorient it towards principles of love, truth, and service—not as external impositions, but as the very pathways to our own flourishing.

3. It is the **active relinquishing of the need to control every outcome**. Just as the artisan surrenders to the grain of the wood, we surrender to the underlying order, trusting that our best efforts, aligned with this greater design, will yield fruits beyond our solitary capacity.

As Thomas à Kempis counsels: "A man must strive to be delivered from self-will, and so be drawn to the truth, and be established in the true light."

This striving is not a battle against self, but a gradual, persistent re-education of the will, gently guiding it back to its true home.

This discipline of fidelity is **the anti-nihilist alternative**. It provides the transcendent anchor that stabilizes the self against the abyss. The soul finds its ultimate liberty not in rejecting all structure, but in voluntarily binding itself to the most perfect structure available. The peace offered is not the restless, fleeting pride of the Übermensch, forever creating and uncreating its own unstable reality, but the deep, sustained stability of one who knows they are moving with the grain of the universe.

This path of spiritual discipline and surrender re-establishes the moral center of gravity, confirming that the Compass is not lost, but merely waiting to be reoriented toward its true North. In this intentional alignment, **the yearning for Theosis begins to be fulfilled, not through aggressive assertion, but through humble, enduring participation**. The world, no longer an existential battlefield, transforms into a grand, purposeful dance.

To Reclaim Ground: A Rooted Guide for Chapter 3

The Hearth (Cooking/Baking)	The Soundtrack (Instrumental)
Make:	**Listen:**
Cornish Pasty (Non-Traditional Fish/Sweet Variation): The rugged exterior holds complex, contrasting fillings, mirroring the complex moral life housed within the resolute Knight Errant.	**Richard Wagner, Rienzi Overture:** The epitome of heroic action and unwavering moral assertion, symbolizing the Knights actively fighting against chaos.
Beef and Seaweed Stew (Cawl Bwyd Môr): The beef provides the Knight's strength, and the seaweed (laverbread) represents deep roots, regional fidelity, and an ancient, enduring moral base	**Aaron Copland, Appalachian Spring:** Represents moral clarity, simplicity, and the foundational hope of a just, non-corruptible community.
The Sweet Pasty (Figgy Hobbin): A dessert take that adds a layer of gentle grace and quiet charity (stoicism warmed by charity).	**Ralph Vaughan Williams, Fantasia on a Theme by Thomas Tallis:** A deeply contemplative meditation on the solemn, internal code of honor and enduring truth.

To Reclaim Ground: A Rooted Guide for Chapter 3 (cont.)

The Hearth (Cooking/Baking)	The Soundtrack (Instrumental)
Make:	Listen:
Aged Farmhouse Cheddar and Dark Cherry Preserves: The Cheddar represents time-tested moral fidelity and enduring strength (the Knight's code). The dark, complex cherry preserve offers a moment of intense, hard-won spiritual quest and depth, matching Coltrane's "Resolution."	**John Coltrane – "Resolution" Heroic Quest:** John Coltrane's "Resolution" embodies an intense, hard-won spiritual quest and profound depth.
Simple Rye Crispbread with Smoked Trout Pâté: The Rye Crispbread is a humble, structured carrier. The Smoked Trout Pâté is richly concentrated and savory, requiring deep, focused savoring. This pairing embodies introspection and melodic fidelity, mirroring the precise, disciplined structure of Weber's "Seriously Deep."	**Eberhard Weber Colours – "Seriously Deep" Focused Introspection:** Eberhard Weber Colours' "Seriously Deep" mirrors the precise, disciplined structure of focused introspection and melodic fidelity.
A Small, Warm Muffin or Scone with Clotted Cream and Heather Honey: This is pure, unpretentious, home-centered comfort. The warmth and simple sweetness capture the "Sentimental Mood"—the warm, human core that drives the moral code and reminds the Knight of what he is fighting to protect.	**Duke Ellington – "In a Sentimental Mood"** The warmth and simple sweetness capture the "Sentimental Mood"—the warm, human core that drives the moral code and reminds the Knight of what he is fighting to protect

Chapter 3 - Knights Errant
Justice and Fidelity in the Void

We have charted the abyss and named the shadows that darken the soul. The diagnosis is complete: the breakdown of meaning leads not to absolute freedom, but to absolute isolation. The response to this fragmentation, then, cannot be an abstract theory or a political platform. It must be a living answer to chaos: a man or a woman of action.

This chapter is a chronicle of courage. Courage is not the absence of fear, but the choice to ignore it when morally compelled. Here, we explore those steady souls who uphold an ethical standard not for guaranteed success or applause, but simply because it is right.

They are the modern Knights Errant: individuals who find meaning not in external validation, but in fidelity to an internal code. Operating in the void of a cynical world, their light is the duty they fulfill.

The light returns—not in triumph, but in duty fulfilled.

The Detective's Code
(Ross & John D. MacDonald)

Moral confusion thrives in the shadow of half-truths, whispers of convenience, and the seductive comfort of plausible deniability. The first, foundational act of the modern knight is therefore the stubborn, relentless pursuit of Truth. This is the vocation of the detective, and it is a profoundly moral vocation—a commitment to stripping away illusion to reveal the unvarnished contours of reality, however uncomfortable.

We look to the hard-boiled realism of the detective genre—not for its violence, but for its uncompromising ethical compass and its practical methodology for navigating moral wildernesses. Writers like Ross MacDonald (particularly in novels such as The Chill or The Goodbye Look) and John D. MacDonald (with his iconic Travis McGee series, perhaps The Deep Blue Good-by or A Tan and Sandy Silence) present us with solitary figures navigating worlds soaked in cynicism and compromise. Their protagonists— Lew Archer or Travis McGee—are not infallible heroes; they are simply men who refuse to let the simple fact be obscured by the convenient lie. They embody a gritty, quiet heroism rooted in intellectual and moral honesty.

The detective's code is stripped down, procedural, and profoundly spiritual in its application, offering a practical pathway for the modern knight:

1. Observe: Look Past the Facade. Go beyond the easy explanation, the public narrative, the convenient story. This demands a disciplined detachment, a refusal to accept surface appearances. It is the practice of seeing what is, not merely what is presented. It requires a profound patience and a cultivated skepticism towards all received wisdom until personally verified.

2. Act with Integrity: Maintain Your Price—Zero. In a world where every principle seems commodified, the detective stands as a fixed point. His personal integrity is his only currency, his unassailable core. This means resisting the subtle corrosions of self-interest, popular opinion, and the siren call of easy compromise. It is an unyielding commitment to an internal compass, even when all external markers are spinning wildly.

3. Seek the Fact: The Truth is the Only Solid Ground. However small, however painful, however inconvenient, the truth is the sole foundation upon which any genuine order—personal or societal—can be built. The detective's work is an archaeological dig through layers of deceit, always searching for the bedrock of reality. This isn't about judgment; it's about clarity. It's about insisting on reality even when reality insists on being ugly.

This process is deliberate, observant, and empathetic—it is the moral clarity of the working knight. The detective knows that justice is often impossible, but truth-seeking is always possible. He is a chronicler of courage who understands that the first step to restoring any kind of order is to name the reality of the situation accurately. He finds sanctity in service not by performing grand, theatrical acts, but by being the one reliable point in a field of deceit. The work is less about arresting the villain and more about clearing the fog so that the innocent can finally see, and the path forward, however arduous, becomes visible. This relentless pursuit of factual clarity, even in the face of overwhelming obfuscation, is the profound service the modern knight offers to a world drowning in willful blindness.

The Code of the Rider
(Louis L'Amour, Hondo)

When the social structure fails entirely—when the law is absent, corrupt, or irrelevant—the foundation of order must reside solely within the individual. This is the stark, moral landscape of the Western, and it gives us the perfect archetype for the Knight Errant: The Code of the Rider. It is here that we find the most visceral, unvarnished expression of a self-authored but divinely aligned ethical compass.

In the narratives of Louis L'Amour (novels such as Hondo, Shalako, or The Walking Drum), the frontier is not merely a geographic location; it is a metaphysical proving ground. There are no courts, no police, and no external validation for doing good, only the harsh judgment of the wilderness and the immediate consequences of one's choices. Yet, the rider operates by an unwavering personal responsibility—a self-imposed code of conduct forged in the crucible of necessity and conscience. He is the solitary figure who finds meaning not in external validation, but in unbending fidelity to an internal code, directly contrasting the nihilistic fear of the void. His entire being becomes a testament to an unwritten law, etched not in stone, but in character.

His actions are the core essence of the Knight Errant, a practical guide to maintaining moral gravity when all external forces seek to pull it apart:

1. He protects the innocent not for reward, but because they are helpless. This is not a calculated heroism, but an instinctive response to vulnerability, born from a deep-seated recognition of shared humanity. It is the practical application of radical empathy in a brutal world.

2. He keeps his word not because of a contract, but because his honor is the only currency he possesses. His integrity is his fixed star. In a world where trust is rare and betrayal common, his reliability is a force of nature, building a micro-cosmos of order around him. His promise is an unbreakable bond, not a transactional agreement.

3. He upholds an ethical standard when societal laws fail. When the letter of the law is broken or non-existent, he lives by its spirit. This requires a constant internal vigilance, a clarity of discernment that transcends the immediate allure of self-preservation or retribution. He becomes the living embodiment of the justice that ought to be.

This code is characterized by quiet honor and a profound aversion to pretense. It is stoicism warmed by active charity. The rider doesn't give speeches about philosophy; he simply acts, his choices defining his creed. He makes the active, moral choice to uphold an ethical standard in the vacuum of a hostile, chaotic world. His strength comes not from brute force, but from the deep knowledge that his actions are aligned with an enduring moral reality, regardless of whether anyone else is watching or whether he lives to see the dawn. He is the living refutation of the nihilist's claim that without God, everything is permitted. The rider knows that without external law, everything is chosen, and that choice becomes the ultimate crucible of character.

This steadfast fidelity—this refusal to descend into the local chaos and instead to embody a higher order—is what defines true moral agency in the void. It is the practical demonstration that self-imposed order, rooted in an unshakeable inner compass, can indeed create islands of meaning and dignity in the most desolate of landscapes, charting a path for others to follow, not by doctrine, but by example.

The Quiet Healer
(James Herriot, All Creatures Great and Small)

After confronting the loud chaos of moral corruption and the quiet violence of the frontier, we must now turn to the most profound act of courage: care. Virtue is not only found in the dramatic defense of law or the solitary assertion of honor; it is equally, if not more powerfully, manifested in the daily, humble ritual of sanctity in service. This is where the grand philosophies become incarnate, where the pursuit of truth and fidelity finds its most tangible and healing expression.

For this, we observe the life chronicled by the veterinarian James Herriot in All Creatures Great and Small. Herriot's world—the bustling, muddy life of the Yorkshire Dales—is devoid of philosophical grandeur, yet rich with moral purpose. His days are a relentless sequence of cold mornings, thankless labor, difficult judgment calls, and the constant, inescapable presence of suffering. He is the quiet healer who finds the sacred not in abstract ideals, but in the intensely ordinary, the immediate, and the often unglamorous. He reveals that true meaning is often found not in towering achievements, but in the persistent, loving engagement with the concrete realities of life.

What Herriot practices is a form of moral realism steeped in practical charity. He possesses no illusions of grand systemic change. He cannot fix the grinding poverty of the farmers, the indifferent cruelty of nature, or the ultimate, inescapable fact of death. His arena of influence is deliberately small: one sick cow, one desperate lamb, one worried owner. Yet, he approaches each with steadfast, humane attention, offering his full skill and presence. This isn't naive idealism; it's a grounded, pragmatic form of compassion that asks: "What can be done right here, right now, for this particular being?"

Moral heroism is not achieving grand, sweeping success; it is the unwavering refusal to turn away from the messy reality of the immediate need. It is the disciplined choice to engage with the pain directly in front of you, even when the odds are stacked, the conditions are grim, and the gratitude is uncertain. This is the essence of grace made visible, stripped of all sentimentality. It demands grit—the willingness to get your hands dirty, to lose sleep, to face frustration, and to sometimes fail publicly. But it is always warmed by grace—the empathetic understanding that suffering is universal and that our highest, most redemptive calling is simply to lighten the burden of another, be they human or animal, with attentive presence and skilled effort.

The quiet healer teaches us that fidelity is not an abstract allegiance to a code; it is the unflinching dedication to the being directly in front of you. This profound focus on the immediate, tangible act of service provides a sanctuary from cynicism, a refuge from the isolating despair of the abyss. In the simple, repetitive acts of healing and caring, the world is made momentarily whole, piece by piece, life by life. The heart, previously hardened by the abyss of unmoored intellect or the chaos of the void, begins to soften and finds its necessary place in **the great chain of being**.

This is the practical path to Theosis through active love: finding connection not in grand pronouncements, but in humble, persistent service. It is the restoration of meaning, not through philosophical argument, but through the embodied virtue of selfless care. The Knight of Care reminds us that true transcendence is often found not in rising above the world, but in bending down to mend its broken parts, one small, compassionate act at a time.

The Architect of the Invisible
(Italo Calvino, Invisible Cities)

We end this chronicle of courage by stepping away from the tangible world of dust and duty toward the realm of imagination. For the final, essential answer to the fragmentation of the modern mind is not only to act rightly, but to see rightly. The Knight Errant must possess not only a strong arm and a steady will, but a mind capable of perceiving the invisible architecture of meaning that undergirds the visible world—the very scaffolding of truth and value that persists even when obscured.

Italo Calvino, in his enchanting work Invisible Cities, provides the indispensable framework for this final ascent. The book is structured as a conversation between the aging explorer Marco Polo and the emperor Kublai Khan, describing cities that may or may not exist. These are not merely fanciful places; they are profound meditations on memory, desire, meaning, and fragility. Crucially, they are a practical guide to the moral imagination's power to construct and sustain reality. Polo's descriptions teach us that the cities we inhabit are as much products of our internal convictions as they are of brick and stone.

The cities that Marco Polo describes are a profound metaphor for the moral imagination as an act of faith and a continuous, active construction. Just as the human mind projects order, memory, and hope onto a random collection of streets and stones, so too does the faithful soul project meaning, purpose, and sanctity onto a world that, left to its own devices, might appear cold and indifferent. This is not naive fantasy, but a radical act of will—a conscious decision to perceive the inherent dignity and potential for goodness that often lies beneath the surface of chaos and despair. The architect of the invisible is the one who understands that the soul is perpetually building its city—a reality constructed not of concrete, but of conviction, sustained by the very act of its envisioning.

The choice, then, is not between meaning and meaninglessness, but between building a city of despair or one of profound, sustaining hope. This profound insight turns our narrative back toward wonder. After the diagnostic darkness of Chapter 2, and the procedural grit of the first three sections of Chapter 3, Calvino reminds us that transcendence is always available to the mind that seeks it, capable of perceiving the sacred infrastructure that reason alone cannot apprehend.

The very capacity to imagine a better, truer, more ordered city—a new Jerusalem—is our greatest, most powerful act of fidelity. It is the the human spirit refusing to be constrained by the current state of the fallen world, actively participating in its renewal. This Lamp Carried Forward is the light of this moral imagination. It is the internal blueprint that guides action and sustains hope.

It is what allows the detective to observe and seek the fact, envisioning a world where truth matters. It is what empowers the rider to uphold his code, imagining a justice beyond the reach of lawlessness. And it is what compels the healer to offer care, perceiving the inherent worth of every suffering creature. They act rightly because they can imagine a world where right action eventually wins, where dignity can be restored, and where individual goodness contributes to a larger, invisible tapestry of meaning. This final note of steadfastness is the recognition that integrity is the continuous, quiet act of carrying that lamp, illuminating the way for oneself and others, and perpetually building the invisible city in the collective human soul.

Transitional Meditation: The Lamp Carried Forward

The journey through the void is complete. We have seen that the human answer to chaos is not a retreat into cynicism, but a commitment to an internal, self-imposed standard of justice and care. These figures—the detached investigator, the quiet rider, the muddy healer, and the hopeful architect—are all performing the same essential task: upholding the invisible code. They are the living evidence that moral order is not a relic, but a constant, active choice. Their work lights the way forward.

To Reclaim Ground: A Rooted Guide for Chapter 4

The Hearth (Cooking/Baking)	The Soundtrack (Instrumental)
Make:	Listen:
Homemade Cheese and Shallot Bread: The act of building something robust and communal from simple elements (flour, cheese, shallots).	**Classical: Bach – Mass in B Minor: "Et in terra pax" (And on Earth, Peace):** The ultimate expression of order, beauty, and fundamental tranquility.
Roast Chicken with Herbs and 40 Cloves of Garlic: An abundant, deeply comforting meal that symbolizes provision, warmth, and the established "Ordered Hearth."	**Classical: Dvořák – Symphony No. 9 ("From the New World"):** A musical journey of longing, discovery, and the profound beauty of building a hopeful future.
Apple and Prune Gallette: A humble, rustic dessert emphasizing simple, nourishing creation and the grace found in the small act of sharing.	**Jazz / Instrumental: Eric Gales – Morning Glory:** A bright, energetic piece suggesting the fresh commitment and new day that comes with finding purpose.
Toasted Challah and Salmon Spread: The braided bread symbolizes the structure and order of creation, paired with a savory, enduring spread that reflects the organic complexity and lasting joy of rebuilding a meaningful life.	**Jazz / Instrumental: Egberto Gismonti – "Água e Vinho" (Water and Wine):** Lyrical, acoustic, and intricate. A piece that feels both technically masterful and profoundly organic, embodying the craftsman-poet building beauty from elemental components.

Chapter 4 - Reclaiming Ground
Building, Resisting, Finding Purpose

We have descended into the abyss and chronicled the quiet courage of those who uphold the code in the void. Now, we begin the work of reclaiming ground. This is the shift from diagnosis to construction, from the code of the knight to the craft of the builder. The true measure of our recovery is not found in a brilliant philosophical system, but in the simplest, most enduring acts: in the care of a garden, the repair of a broken hinge, the ritual of bread rising on a kitchen counter.

The soul, like a neglected house, cannot be repaired by argument alone. It requires the slow, patient, and intensely incarnational effort of a craftsman. We must become those who knead ideas like dough—feeling the texture, understanding the weight, waiting for the necessary rise. The goal is not cheap comfort, but a consolation earned, a deep peace shot through with the hard-won joy of having stared at the ruin and chosen to rebuild.

Meaning Amid Ruin
(Viktor Frankl, Man's Search for Meaning)

Our work begins at the point of greatest existential pressure: suffering. If the abyss teaches us anything, it is that life will inevitably place us in situations where all external structures—safety, predictability, dignity—are stripped away. It is here, in the rubble, that we discover the ultimate, unassailable freedom chronicled by Viktor Frankl in Man's Search for Meaning.

Frankl's core insight, born in the unimaginable degradation of the concentration camps, is that the last of the human freedoms is the ability to choose one's attitude in any given set of circumstances. Though the body may be chained, the inner will remains sovereign. This is freedom through interior consent.

When you cannot change the circumstance, you are challenged to change yourself. The question shifts from Why is this happening to me? to **What is required of me in this moment?**

Life asks the questions, and we answer with our existence. This realization is profoundly redemptive. It teaches us that **suffering is not a senseless void**, but a potential forge for meaning. It forces us to confront **the Will to Meaning—the innate human drive to find purpose, even amid ruin**. This is not mere stoicism; it is an act of creation. By choosing a response of dignity, fidelity, or courage in the face of pain, we are actively injecting meaning into a meaningless situation.

This understanding is the anchor for our ascent. It assures us that our interior temple is utterly defensible. No circumstance, no external force, and no amount of cynicism can take away the power of that final, sovereign choice.

The Moral Law Restored
(C.S. Lewis, Mere Christianity)

With our interior freedom secured, we must now address the architecture of the moral landscape. Our recovery requires not just an inner attitude, but a rational framework—a set of blueprints that define the structure of the good life. For this, we turn to the clear, uncompromising, and supremely rational faith presented by C.S. Lewis in Mere Christianity.

Lewis, the reluctant convert, guides us back to the great, enduring truth: the Moral Law is not a set of arbitrary rules handed down by a jealous deity, but a description of how reality is built. Just as there are laws of physics that govern the external world (gravity, motion), there are laws of human nature that govern the internal world (justice, fairness, compassion). To violate these laws is not merely to be naughty; it is to misunderstand and break the self. He gives us a rational faith that serves as the road home.

The Moral Law is the music of the universe; our job is to find the right pitch.

This idea is the ultimate source of consolation earned. Lewis takes the anxiety and intellectual fragmentation of the modern condition and systematically shows how the greatest human longings—for justice, for meaning, for connection—point inevitably toward a transcendent designer. He strips away the sentimentality and leaves us with a choice based on evidence and reason.

The Ordered Hearth—our home, our work, our relationships—cannot stand if it is built on shifting philosophical sand. Lewis provides the square, true foundation. He allows us to build with confidence because we are not inventing the moral ground; we are discovering it. This is the rebuilding of the domestic temple, where every act of kindness and every commitment to truth is an alignment with the universal, sustaining rhythm.

Grace in Blood
(Flannery O'Connor, A Good Man Is Hard to Find)

The transition from a rational framework to a lived reality of faith often requires a violent shock. The peace we seek is not found in an easy surrender, but in a crisis that shatters the protective shell of the ego. For this necessary, painful confrontation, we turn to the unflinching genius of Flannery O'Connor. Her stories are not comforting parables; they are moments of Grace in Blood. O'Connor's world, as seen in stories like A Good Man Is Hard to Find, is dark, gothic, and often brutal.

She believed that to reach the spiritually deaf, you have to shout and sometimes even hit them with a two-by-four. Her antagonists and her protagonists are often arrogant, self-deluded, and deeply flawed. Redemption, when it comes, is not a gentle invitation; it is a violent intrusion. It is the shock of grace.

The truth is revealed not in the pleasant afternoon sermon, but at the point of ultimate distress.

The moment of crisis in her work serves as the hinge—the sudden, terrifying transition from the prison of the self to the possibility of transformation. Only when the character's worldly pride and comfortable illusions are completely dismantled does the genuine opening for grace appear. This is not a philosophy of despair; it is a brutal statement of hope: only radical pain can sometimes yield radical redemption.

This is a necessary element of our redemptive arc. **The peace we are building is hard-won joy.** It must account for the reality of evil and the depth of human corruption. O'Connor teaches us that the incarnational life is not merely picturesque; it is often painful, messy, and requires a complete spiritual surrender that feels, in the moment, like death. It confirms that the road home is paved with difficulty, but the destination is absolute.

The Ordered Hearth
(Edith Wharton, The House of Mirth)

To speak of rebuilding the domestic temple and the virtue of order, we must first examine the high cost of sacrificing inner foundation for external façade. We learn this lesson not from a sermon, but from the searing tragedy observed by Edith Wharton in The House of Mirth.

Wharton's protagonist, Lily Bart, is a woman of exquisite grace and refinement, trained only for the spectacle of high society. She is a structure of beauty built on air, possessing every outward elegance but lacking any inward substance—no true vocation, no stable commitment, and no personal moral law beyond the shifting currents of social opinion. Her life is a pursuit of external validation, and her eventual ruin is the ultimate diagnosis of a soul that failed to build a proper foundation.

The book is a stark warning that beauty without foundation is a liability. The Ordered Hearth is not about having an immaculate house; it is about having an immaculate interior intention. It is the daily discipline of choosing fidelity over convenience and substance over surface.

If the soul is merely a mirror reflecting the desires of the crowd, it will shatter when the crowd turns away.

This section serves as a practical, cautionary contrast to Lewis's Moral Law. You can know the Law intellectually, but if your daily life is merely a frantic attempt to maintain a false external image, your inner structure will fail, just as surely as an architecturally unsound building collapses. The work of reclaiming ground means prioritizing the integrity of the hidden things: the honest budget, the maintained relationships, the quiet prayer at dusk, the commitment to an honest day's work.

This patient, often unseen work is the true resistance against the cynical, superficial spirit of the age. We are not just building houses; we are building souls that can withstand the storm.

Bread of Creation
(James Beard, Beard on Bread)

We culminate this chapter of redemption with the most elemental and redemptive act of all: creation with your own hands. We move from the philosophical and the psychological to the intensely tangible, finding the sanctity of craft and domestic liturgy in the kitchen, guided by the warmth and authority of James Beard and his foundational work, Beard on Bread.

Why bread?

Because the act of making bread—the slow mixing, the patient kneading of the dough, the required waiting for the rise, and the transformative heat of the oven—is a perfect, ancient analogy for the work of the soul.

The baker embodies the craftsman-poet. He works not with abstract ideas, but with gravity, temperature, yeast, and flour. He understands the simple yet profound truth that meaning is found in the making.

1. Patience: The baker cannot rush the yeast. He must wait, submitting his will to the pace of natural creation. This mirrors the freedom through interior consent taught by Frankl.

2. Transformation: The heat of the oven takes four disparate elements and transforms them into something wholly new, sustaining, and beautiful. This is the definition of redemptive work.

3. Intimacy: The final product—bread shared at the table—is the ultimate act of vocation and home. It is the physical manifestation of love and provision.

Every deliberate, ordinary act—making coffee, repairing a gate, kneading dough—is an opportunity to inject purpose into the world.

This final image re-enchanting the ordinary world. **The Bread of Creation** is the embodiment of the entire chapter: the grand philosophical truths of Lewis and Frankl are made real and digestible. **The act of bringing something good and true into existence with intention is the highest form of reclaiming ground.**

It is a small, quiet, daily victory over the despair and fragmentation of the void. It is the deep peace of knowing that your hands have contributed something beautiful and necessary to the world.

To Reclaim Ground: A Rooted Guide for Our Conclusion -

Handholds for the Journey's End

The Hearth (Cooking/Baking) Make:	The Soundtrack (Instrumental) Listen:
Tea and Cucumber, Cream Cheese, and Watercress Sandwiches: Light, elegant, and simple fare—the perfect, humble ceremonial food for quiet reflection and social grace.	**Classical: Erik Satie - Gymnopédie No. 1:** Luminous, still, and minimal piano music, creating the meditative space required for integration.
Small Loaf of Sweet Bread or Brioche: A simple, nourishing, and slightly comforting baked good, symbolizing the final, shared fruit of the journey.	**Classical: Gregorian Chant - Ubi Caritas et Amor (Where Charity and Love Are):** A sacred, pure melody that centers the final reflection on love, the ultimate Moral Law.
Crème de Menthe Syllabub: The act of whipping air into the syllabub's sustained, light structure parallels the constant, quiet work of Ceaseless Prayer. Its cool, minty clarity embodies the reward of finding serenity and stillness within the continuous rhythm of life.	**Jazz / Instrumental: Jaco Pastorius - "Continuum":** A solo/trio piece featuring a sustained, lyrical, and meditative bass line, suggesting the enduring path and the "handholds" of the long journey.
Blue Cheese and Honey Shortbread: The deliberate pairing of the sharp, complex blue cheese with the simple, calming sweetness of honey forces a concentrated focus on balance and harmony. This is the final, contemplative act, where the soul finds Glory in the Now by accepting the world's contrasting nature as one complete, beautiful reality.	**Jazz / Instrumental: Bill Evans Trio - Waltz for Debby:** Elegant, introspective, and gentle jazz that captures serenity and reflection without finality.

Conclusion
Handholds for the Journey's End

We have reached the summit of our ascent. The path has led us through wonder and shadow, through the intellectual pride of the void and the quiet heroism of duty. Now, all that remains is to stop, to breathe, and to integrate. The structure is built; the compass is set. This final chapter is not about grand pronouncements, but about providing handholds—simple, rhythmic practices that ground the great, enduring truths in the fabric of your everyday life.

The world is not saved by arguments, but by the slow, consecrated acts of attention.

Here, the noise of philosophy fades, and the sound of a single bell rings in the mountain pass: still, sacred, and crystalline. This is the serenity earned after the motion, the point where practicing presence, prayer, and creative grace become one continuous act.

1. The Consecration of the Mundane
(Brother Lawrence, Practice of the Presence of God)

If the world is a gift (Chesterton) and meaning is found in service (Herriot), then no act is too small to be significant. Brother Lawrence, the humble cook and lay brother, understood this truth better than most. His life was a continuous spiritual exercise: finding God not in lofty contemplation, but in the simple duty of the kitchen.

This is the antidote to fragmentation: **the refusal to mentally compartmentalize the sacred.**

Your life is not divided into "spiritual time" and "work time." Every task—washing a dish, answering an email, tying a shoe—is an opportunity for fidelity. When you perform a mundane task with complete, quiet attention, you are doing more than simply completing an action. You are consecrating the mundane. You are testifying that this moment, this chore, holds as much value as any prayer.

Practice: Before undertaking a task, pause for three breaths. State your intention: "I will do this task—this folding, this driving, this calculating—with complete attention, as an act of service." Let the rhythm of the work become the rhythm of your peace.

2. Ceaseless Prayer
(The Way of a Pilgrim)

To navigate the cynicism of the void, the soul needs an interior sanctuary that is always open, always accessible. This sanctuary is built through ceaseless prayer. As illustrated in the Russian spiritual classic, The Way of a Pilgrim, this practice is not complicated liturgy; it is the rhythmic, repetitive centering of the Heart.
The pilgrim found his peace in the Jesus Prayer ("Lord Jesus Christ, Son of God, have mercy on me, a sinner") whispered continuously, synchronizing it with the beat of his heart and the rhythm of his breathing. The content of the words matters, but the rhythm matters more. It is a spiritual drill that re-establishes the Moral Law (Lewis) deep within the biological core.

Practice: Choose a simple phrase—a word of gratitude, a petition for peace, or a traditional short prayer. Assign it to a physical routine: the walking of your feet, the washing of your hands, or the brewing of your morning coffee. Let the mantra become a spiritual current, always flowing beneath the surface of your thoughts, protecting your center of gravity (Epictetus).

3. The Holy Conversation
(Martin Buber, Tales of the Hasidim)

If meaning is relational, it must be found in the space between people. The anti-nihilist, having mastered the self, must learn to meet the other not as an object to be used or an obstacle to be managed, but as a fully realized, sacred presence.

Martin Buber called this the I-Thou relationship. In Buber's tales, the Hasidic masters understood that every true encounter is a moment of redemption. When we look at another person—truly see them—we are not observing a type or a role; we are entering a Holy Conversation.

The nihilistic impulse is to reduce the other to an I-It—a colleague, a customer, a function. The Will to Fidelity (à Kempis) compels us to choose the difficult, open posture of the I-Thou. This takes courage, for true presence makes us vulnerable. It requires the deep humility to set aside our own agenda and receive the person as a complete world unto themselves.

Practice: In your next conversation, commit the first two minutes to listening without forming your reply. Observe the other person's face, the tone of their voice, and the weight of their words. Let their existence be a momentary priority over your own. This simple act of attentiveness heals the fragmentation between souls.

4. Glory in the Now
(Bashō, Selected Haiku)

After the great movements of the journey, we settle into the still point—the recognition that eternity is not found in the distant future, but in the compressed reality of the present moment. The Japanese poet Bashō achieved this visionary presence in his Haiku. He found Glory in the Now by observing nature with absolute clarity and poetic precision.

Old pond ... A frog jumps in. Sound of water.

A universe unfolds in three lines. Bashō teaches us that the world is perpetually offering us the gift of existence (Chesterton), but we are usually too busy debating tomorrow to accept it. The practice of creative grace is nothing more than the profound decision to see the ordinary as luminous.

Practice: Pause your movement. Choose one small, visible detail near you—a crack in the pavement, the dust motes in the light, the steam from a hot cup. Stare at it until your brain stops naming it and starts experiencing it. Let that single detail hold the weight and wonder of the entire cosmos. That moment of clarity is your access point to the enduring.

A Rule for the Anti-Nihilist

The path is defined by a commitment to small, corrective choices that constantly reorient the Compass toward truth and stability. Let this litany serve as your Rule for the Anti-Nihilist—the spiritual mechanics of a life rebuilt.

1. Pray when bored: To consecrate the vacancy with presence.

2. Bake when angry: To transform destructive heat into constructive, shared creation.

3. Read when lost: To anchor the soul in enduring wisdom rather than circulating error.

4. Serve when proud: To practice humility and find sanctity in the needs of the other.

Thus, the soul rebuilds the world.

To Reclaim Ground- A Rooted Guide

Epilogue The Map Folded Back

The Hearth (Cooking/Baking) Make:	The Soundtrack (Instrumental) Listen:
Turkey Tetrazzini: A classic casserole of leftovers, symbolizing the culmination of the entire journey. It's warm, comforting, and wholly unpretentious—a true celebration of sustained, earned sustenance.	**Classical: Ralph Vaughan Williams - The Lark Ascending:** Embodies pure, effortless transcendence and soaring, unburdened peace, representing the soul's final, gentle lift.
A Crust of Bread, Époisses, Stilton, and Pedro Ximénez Sherry/Wine: A contemplative finale. The crust represents the elemental beginning, the cheeses, complex maturity, and the P.X. sherry, the richness and maturity of reflection.	**Classical: Arvo Pärt - Cantus in Memory of Benjamin Britten:** Deeply solemn and beautiful, creating a sense of restorative closure and serene contemplation.
Single Whitefish Shumai with Yuzu Sauce and Shiitake/ Kombu Dusting: A single, meticulously crafted item that embodies final cleansing clarity. The umami-rich dusting anchors the piece, symbolizing the enduring, humble ground.	**Jazz / Instrumental: John Coltrane - "After the Rain":** The sonic metaphor for the chapter's title. A quiet, meditative ballad signifying cleansing, calm, and clarity after the storm.
Cherry-Glazed Duck Breast on Grilled Pumpernickel (Mignardise Salée): A complex, dark flavor profile that provides a deliberate callback to the abyss (Chapter 2), now transformed into a rich, comforting, and earned reward—the savory memory of the journey's intensity.	**Jazz / Instrumental: Pat Metheny - "James":** A beautiful, lyrical piece filled with warm nostalgia and quiet, shimmering hope, serving as a gentle, positive resolution.

To Reclaim Ground- A Rooted Guide
Epilogue The Map Folded Back
Alternate

Alternative Epilogue Celebration: For those who truly wish to anchor themselves in the heart of domestic abundance after such a rigorous pilgrimage, we offer a celebratory, unapologetic indulgence: **A Whole Turkey Stuffed with Oyster Dressing.**

This is the ultimate rejection of nihilism: the full, comforting weight of tradition, family, and home, enjoyed not out of necessity, but as a deliberate and magnificent celebration of having found your way back to the table. Go forth and feast.

Listening?

Track / Artist	Theme	Rationale for Pairing
Phase Dance by Pat Metheny Group	The Earned Rhythm	A flowing, structured, and joyous instrumental piece that symbolizes the rhythm and grace found in a fully established, intentional life.
First Circle by Pat Metheny Group	The Completed Cycle	An expansive, driving piece with powerful, repetitive cycles that musically convey the sense of completion, security, and return to the established home.

To Reclaim Ground- A Rooted Guide

Track / Artist	Theme	Rationale for Pairing
Nessun Dorma (Vocal by Pavarotti/Bocelli/ etc.)	The Break/The Magnificent	A deliberate break from the instrumental rule. This piece is pure, magnificent human passion and triumph, an unapologetic expression of the joy found in the return to abundance.
Old Train by Tony Rice	The Grounded End	The final, simple, and masterful acoustic bluegrass track. It is humble, technical, and profoundly rooted in the American soil and tradition, embodying the ultimate comfort of the journey's end.

Epilogue
The Map Folded Back

The compass is set. The hearth is warm. Our journey through these pages, from the foundational ascent to the quiet grace of the final Rule, has reached its natural end.

This book was never meant to be a destination. It was, rather, a map—a temporary tool drawn up to remind you of things you already knew: the reliable architecture of the moral universe, the immovable strength of your own inner will, and the steady, redemptive light found in ordinary acts of fidelity.

Look down at the path before you. The concepts we explored—Wonder as Sanity, the Discipline of Fortitude, the shock of grace, the bread of creation—are not theories to be memorized; they are the terrain itself. You do not carry the map through the mountains. You carry the map to the trailhead, and then you begin to walk. The map was only meant to bring you to the road.

Our voices—mine and those of the companions we summoned, from Epictetus to James Beard—must now grow quiet. The teacher returns to silence. **You have been given the Compass of intentionality and the blueprint for the Hearth of order.** You have the tools to practice presence and to resist the spirit of fragmentation. All doctrine must now be laid aside.

The great work of the anti-nihilist is to trust that the ground is solid, even when the air is thick with doubt. Trust the small, corrective choices. Trust the rhythm of your hands in the work. Trust the silence you cultivate in the morning.

This is the meaning of closure without finality: the book ends, but the true journey of reclaiming ground has only just begun. The task of weaving grace, meaning, and purpose into the day is a perpetual, quiet act of creation.

May your path be steady. May your vision be clear.

May a deep and quiet gratitude fill your spirit for the unearned abundance and beauty woven into the fabric of existence. May your journey be marked by an honoring of this profound givenness, a reverence for the shared human experience, and a steadfast protection against forces that seek to unravel meaning and sow discord. May you find strength in the shared light of community, and may you forever be shielded from the shadows of nihilism and divisive thought.

The map was always meant to disappear in your hands.

All that remains is to walk, and

to
give

thanks.

Appendix: Elemental Recipes

These brief guides are intended not for culinary perfection, but as blueprints for the Incarnational Act–a simple, focused physical exercise to ground the mind before reading.

Irish Soda Bread
(Theme: Unadorned, Foundational Structure)
Act: The mixing of disparate elements into a single, cohesive form.
Ingredients: 3 cups all-purpose flour, 1 tsp baking soda, 1 tsp salt, 1.5 cups buttermilk.
Method: Combine all dry ingredients thoroughly. Make a well in the center and pour in the buttermilk. Mix until a shaggy, cohesive dough forms. Knead very briefly (about 30 seconds). Shape into a round, cut a deep 'X' on top, and bake at 400°F (200°C) for 35-40 minutes until golden and hollow when tapped.

White Bean Dip (Elemental Base)
(Theme: Elemental Sustenance and Accessible First Step)
Act: The humbling of hard ingredients into a simple, nourishing paste.
Ingredients: 1 can Cannellini beans (rinsed/drained), 2-3 cloves garlic, 1/4 cup olive oil, 1 tbsp lemon juice, salt, pepper.
Method: Place the beans, garlic, olive oil, and lemon juice into a food processor. Blend until completely smooth, pausing to scrape the sides. Taste and season generously with salt and pepper. Serve immediately with a crust of bread.

Cream of Mushroom Soup with Endive
(Theme: Earthy Ground meets Sharp Counterpoint)
Act: Building a deep, comforting base, then introducing a sharp, necessary contrast.
Ingredients: 1 lb mushrooms (any mix), 1 shallot, 3 cups vegetable or chicken broth, 1/2 cup heavy cream, 1 head Belgian endive, salt, butter.
Method: Sauté the mushrooms and finely diced shallot in butter until softened. Pour in the broth and simmer gently for 15-20 minutes. Optional: Blend half the soup for desired texture. Stir in the heavy cream. Serve hot, garnished with thinly sliced raw endive leaves to introduce a necessary, bitter contrast.

The Foundational Ascent

Black Cowboy Coffee
(Theme: Unwavering Focus and Pure Energy)
Act: The intentional, non-distracted brewing of a solitary fuel.
Ingredients: Dark roast ground coffee (coarsely ground), water.
Method: Brew coffee (drip, press, or percolator) with a higher ratio of coffee to water than usual. Serve black and potent. The only acceptable additions are the conscious thought of your primary intention and the sound of the chosen music.

Texas Breakfast Hash Chili with Hatch Chiles
(Theme: Fortitude, Drive, and Essential Fire)
Act: The building of a rugged, complex flavor that rewards effort.
Ingredients: Potatoes, ground beef or bison, 1-2 Hatch or Jalapeño chiles (seeded and diced), onion, spices (cumin, chili powder), a fried egg.
Method: Sear the meat and onion. Add diced potatoes and chiles; cook until soft. Season heavily. Serve hot in a bowl, topped with a single, perfectly fried egg for final richness and sustenance.

Ashcakes with Honey and Cayenne
(Theme: Basic, Humble Foundation)
Act: Creating bread from the simplest elements using elemental heat.
Ingredients: 1 cup cornmeal (or coarse flour), 1/2 cup water, pinch of salt.
Toppings: Honey, Cayenne pepper.
Method: Mix ingredients into a thick dough. Form small, flat discs. Cook on a hot, dry, cast-iron skillet (or in foil over embers) until firm and browned. Serve warm, drizzled with Honey for energy and a dash of Cayenne for focus.

Aged Asiago Wedge and Toasted Walnuts
(Theme: Precision, Clarity, and Enduring Structure)
Act: Savoring focused, high-quality simplicity.
Ingredients: 1 small wedge Aged Asiago (grana or stravecchio), a small handful of Walnuts.
Method: Lightly toast the walnuts in a dry pan until fragrant. Break the Asiago into rough, crystalline shards. Savor slowly, alternating between the sharp, granular cheese and the earthy nut.

Square of Olive Oil Cake
(Theme: Deep Roots of Wisdom and Gentle Hope)
Act: Enjoying a simple, ancient form of nourishing cake.
Ingredients: 1 slice of a moist Olive Oil Cake (or pound cake).
Method: Serve the cake at room temperature. The practice here is in the slow savoring of the dense, simple flavor, connecting the taste to the deep, enduring roots of Mediterranean wisdom.

Navigating the Abyss

"Burnt Ends" (Intensely Charred Brisket/Pork Belly)
(Theme: Darkness, Complexity, and Brutal Flavor Profile)
Act: The intentional charring of rich meat to expose complex, smoky depth.
Ingredients: 1 lb beef brisket point or pork belly, BBQ rub (heavy on paprika/brown sugar), BBQ sauce.
Method: Cut meat into cubes. Rub heavily. Slow smoke or roast at low temperature (250°F / 120°C) until very tender. Toss in thick BBQ sauce and roast again at high heat (400°F / 200°C) until the edges are intensely caramelized and charred. This brutal cooking is the key.

Charred Roasted Beet
(Theme: Deeply Grounded Base and Confrontation)
Act: Using high, aggressive heat to reveal the earthiest, darkest flavor of a simple root.
Ingredients: 1-2 medium beets, olive oil, coarse salt.
Method: Toss beets (skin on) in olive oil and salt. Roast at high heat (425°F / 220°C) or grill until the skin is blackened and the edges are aggressively caramelized. Peel the skin (the darkness) to expose the deep red, earthy core. Serve warm.

Dark Rye Bread with Molasses and Black Currants
(Theme: Shadows, Deep Sweetness, and Complex Glimmers)
Act: The patient, required work of building a dense, challenging, yet richly textured structure.
Ingredients: Dark rye flour, bread flour, yeast, blackstrap molasses, black currants (soaked), salt.
Method: Use a slow, overnight rise if possible. The dough will be dense and sticky. The molasses is essential for the color and deep, tar-like flavor. Bake until the crust is very dark and firm. The pockets of tart currants should break up the darkness with sharp flavor.

Knights Errant

Cornish Pasty (Non-Traditional Fish/Sweet Variation)
(Theme: Complex Moral Life in a Rugged Exterior)
Act: Encasing contrasting flavors—savory and sweet—within a resilient, humble shell.
Ingredients: Shortcrust pastry dough. Savory filling (fish, leeks, cream, cheese). Sweet filling (apple, raisins, figs, brown sugar).
Method: Roll dough into large circles. For the savory filling, pre-cook fish/leeks and mix with cream/cheese. For the sweet, mix fruit/sugar/spices. Place filling on one half of the dough, fold over, crimp the edges tightly, and bake at 375°F (190°C) until golden.

Beef and Seaweed Stew (Elemental Cawl)

(Theme: Deep Roots, Regional Fidelity, and Ancient Moral Base)

Act: Slow-cooking robust ingredients to create an uncompromised, enduring source of strength.

Ingredients: Diced beef (stew meat), diced root vegetables (carrots, potatoes), beef stock, laver/laverbread (seaweed puree), herbs.

Method: Sear beef cubes. Add vegetables and stock. Simmer gently (cawl style) until the beef is very tender (2-3 hours). Stir in the laverbread for its deep, ancient flavor, seasoning with only salt and pepper.

The Sweet Pasty (Figgy Hobbin)

(Theme: Gentle Grace and Quiet Charity)

Act: A small, sweet reward emphasizing simple, unpretentious warmth.

Ingredients: Shortcrust pastry dough, filling (apples, dried figs, raisins, brown sugar, cinnamon/nutmeg).

Method: Mix all filling ingredients. Roll dough into small, individual circles. Place filling in the center, fold over to form a semicircle, and crimp. Bake until crust is golden and firm.

Aged Farmhouse Cheddar and Dark Cherry Preserves

(Theme: Time-Tested Fidelity and Hard-Won Quest)

Act: Pairing enduring structural integrity with a complex, dark flavor of spiritual depth.

Ingredients: Aged, sharp Farmhouse Cheddar, high-quality Dark Cherry Preserves.

Method: Slice Cheddar thickly (the structural block). Place a small dollop of the dark, concentrated preserves on the side. Savor the sharp, pure cheese immediately followed by the complex, sweet-tart fruit.

Simple Rye Crispbread with Smoked Trout Pâté

(Theme: Introspection and Disciplined Structure)

Act: A precisely structured, rich, and intensely savory bite requiring focused savoring.

Ingredients: Thin Rye Crispbread, Smoked Trout Pâté (trout, cream cheese, lemon juice, dill).

Method: Prepare a simple pâté. Spread a thin, even layer of the concentrated pâté on the rigid crispbread. This small, focused bite embodies the precision and discipline of the Rider's Code.

A Small, Warm Muffin or Scone with Clotted Cream and Heather Honey

(Theme: Warm Human Core and Home-Centered Comfort)

Act: Enjoying a simple, unpretentious food of pure comfort and provision.

Ingredients: Plain scone or muffin (warmed), Clotted Cream (or thick butter), Heather Honey (or local honey).

Method: Split the warm scone or muffin. Apply a generous amount of cream and a drizzle of honey. The warmth is essential, signaling the protected and established moral core of the hearth.

Reclaiming Ground

Homemade Cheese and Shallot Bread
(Theme: Building Something Robust and Communal)
Act: The patient, intentional work of mixing, kneading, and seeing a complex structure rise.
Ingredients: Bread flour, yeast, water, grated hard cheese (cheddar/gruyère), sautéed shallots, salt.
Method: Form a simple yeast dough. Fold in the cheese and softened shallots during the final kneading. Allow to rise slowly, then bake until deeply golden and fragrant.

Roast Chicken with Herbs and 40 Cloves of Garlic
(Theme: Provision, Warmth, and the Established "Ordered Hearth")
Act: The simple, long-term commitment of providing a celebratory, abundant meal.
Ingredients: 1 whole chicken, fresh herbs (rosemary, thyme), 40 whole, unpeeled garlic cloves, olive oil, salt, pepper.
Method: Rub the chicken heavily with olive oil, salt, and pepper. Stuff the cavity with herbs. Surround the bird with the unpeeled garlic cloves. Roast at a medium heat (375°F / 190°C) until juices run clear. The garlic will become soft and spreadable.

Apple and Prune Gallette
(Theme: Simple, Nourishing Creation and the Grace of Sharing)
Act: Creating a rustic, free-form dessert that emphasizes humility and grace.
Ingredients: Pie crust dough, sliced apples, pitted prunes (or dried apricots), brown sugar, cinnamon, butter.
Method: Roll the dough into a rough, free-form circle. Mound the sliced apples and prunes in the center, leaving a two-inch border. Fold the border over the fruit, brush with butter, and sprinkle with sugar. Bake until crust is crisp and filling is bubbly.

Toasted Challah and Salmon Spread
(Theme: Structure, Order, and Lasting Joy)
Act: Braiding the bread (structure) and preparing a rich spread (complex, enduring flavor).
Ingredients: Sliced Challah bread, smoked salmon, cream cheese, lemon juice, capers, fresh dill.
Method: Toast the Challah until crisp. Whip the cream cheese with diced smoked salmon, lemon juice, and dill. Spread generously onto the warm, braided slices of Challah.

Handholds for the Journey's End

Crème de Menthe Syllabub
(Theme: Enduring Path, Lyrical Handholds)
Act: Creating a light, enduring structure from air and spirit.
Ingredients: Heavy cream, Crème de Menthe, sugar, lemon juice.
Method: Whip the cream until soft peaks form. Gently fold in the liqueurs, sugar, and juice. The resulting structure should be airy yet firm, embodying sustained effort. Chill until ready to serve.

Blue Cheese and Honey Shortbread
(Theme: Serenity and Reflection)
Act: Pairing contrasting flavors (the complex savory vs. the pure sweet) for mature introspection.
Ingredients: Shortbread dough, strong Blue Cheese (crumbled), local Honey (for drizzle).
Method: Prepare a simple shortbread dough. Fold in the crumbled cheese before baking. Serve warm, drizzled with honey. The intense, salty complexity must be balanced by the simple sweetness.

Turkey Tetrazzini
(Theme: Culmination and Sustained, Earned Sustenance)
Act: The resourceful creation of a warming, celebratory, and unpretentious meal from provisions.
Ingredients: Cooked turkey (or chicken), pasta (linguine/spaghetti), cream, parmesan cheese, mushrooms, peas, white wine (optional).
Method: Cook pasta. Sauté mushrooms, add flour and liquid (broth/wine/cream) to make a sauce. Fold in the diced turkey, peas, and parmesan. Combine with pasta, top with cheese, and bake until bubbly and golden.

A Crust of Bread, Époisses, Stilton, and Pedro Ximénez Sherry/Wine
(Theme: Contemplative Finale and Rich Maturity)
Act: A small, highly intentional pairing, savoring the richness earned over time.
Ingredients: Crust of high-quality, artisanal Bread, Époisses (washed-rind cheese), Stilton (blue cheese), Pedro Ximénez (P.X.) Sherry (or sweet wine).
Method: Serve the cheeses at room temperature. The practice is in the slow contemplation of the contrast between the pungent, complex cheeses and the intense, syrupy sweetness of the P.X. sherry.
Single Whitefish Shumai with Yuzu Sauce and Shiitake/Kombu Dusting (Petit Four)

Cleansing Clarity and Enduring Ground

Act: A final, single, perfect bite—a meditative moment of focus.
Ingredients: 1 Whitefish Shumai (steamed), Yuzu juice (mixed with soy), dried Shiitake/Kombu (ground to a dust).
Method: Steam the Shumai until cooked through. Place the single dumpling on a small plate. Drizzle with the Yuzu sauce and dust lightly with the umami powder. Consume slowly, focusing on the single, bright, and deeply grounded flavor.

Cherry-Glazed Duck Breast on Grilled Pumpernickel (Mignardise Salée)

(Theme: Savory Memory of the Journey's Intensity)
Act: Transforming a dark flavor profile (pumpernickel) into a rich, comforting reward.
Ingredients: Thin slice of Duck Breast (seared/cooked), Cherry Reduction (dark, syrupy), Pumpernickel bread (grilled), finely julienned nettles or dandelion greens (garnish).
Method: Slice the duck very thin. Reduce cherry sauce until thick. Grill the pumpernickel bread. Place the duck on the bread, drizzle with the dark reduction, and top with the bitter greens for contrast. Serve as a single, savory bite.

A Whole Turkey Stuffed with Oyster Dressing

(Theme: Celebration and Comfort of the Hearth Restored)
Act: A fully abundant, unashamed celebration of success and the return to the overflowing hearth.
Ingredients: 1 large whole turkey, Oyster Dressing (bread, oysters, herbs, broth).
Method: Stuff the turkey cavity with the dressing. Roast until the skin is golden and the meat is done. This requires a full, dedicated day of effort, symbolizing the completion of the arduous journey and the return to well-earned comfort.

www.ingramcontent.com/pod-product-compliance
Lightning Source LLC
Chambersburg PA
CBHW051321120626
46547CB00015B/2343